Sit & Solve®

BRAINTEASERS

DERRICK NIEDERMAN

PUZZLE
WRIGHT
PRESS

An imprint of Sterling
Publishing Co., Inc.

www.puzzlewright.com

D0205110

Puzzlewright Press, the distinctive Puzzlewright Press logo, and Sit & Solve are
registered trademarks of Sterling Publishing Co., Inc.

2   4   6   8   10   9   7   5   3   1

Published in 2010 by Sterling Publishing Co., Inc.
387 Park Avenue South, New York, NY 10016
© 2003 by Derrick Niederman
Distributed in Canada by Sterling Publishing
c/o Canadian Manda Group, 165 Dufferin Street
Toronto, Ontario, Canada M6K 3H6
Distributed in the United Kingdom by GMC Distribution Services
Castle Place, 166 High Street, Lewes, East Sussex, England BN7 1XU
Distributed in Australia by Capricorn Link (Australia) Pty. Ltd.
P.O. Box 704, Windsor, NSW 2756, Australia

Printed in China

Sterling ISBN 978-1-4027-8021-9

For information about custom editions, special sales, premium and
corporate purchases, please contact Sterling Special Sales
Department at 800-805-5489 or specialsales@sterlingpublishing.com.

CONTENTS

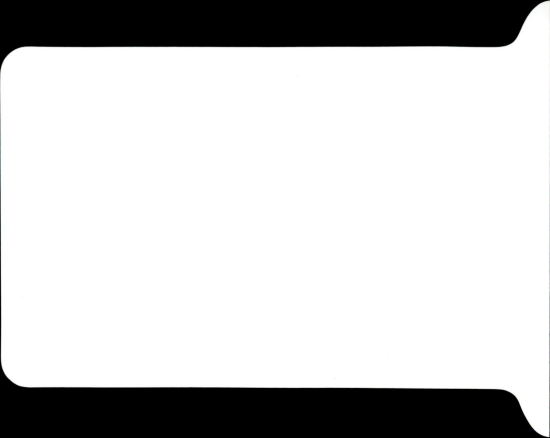

INTRODUCTION

I hope you're sitting down. No, really. Some things are best done sitting down: riding a horse, playing a piano, and, well … doing puzzles, of course. Inside this book you will find over 60 brainteasers, most of which you haven't seen before. How do I know this? Because I conjured up the vast majority of these puzzles myself. Word puzzles, arithmetic puzzles, even puzzles with circles and squares. So keep a pencil handy, and don't forget the chair. How can you give these puzzles a standing ovation if you're not sitting down first?

—Derrick Niederman

1.
THE HARD WAY

In this word ladder, your task is to convert the word PASSER into the word SPARSE, by switching two adjacent letters at a time, in exactly five moves. Write each interim step on one of the blank lines.

P A S S E R

_____

_____

_____

_____

S P A R S E

Answer on page 63.

2.
WHO'S NEXT?

What is the next number in the following sequence?
(There are two possible answers.)

$$17, \quad 19, \quad 23, \quad 29, \quad ?$$

3.
CODE DEPENDENCE

Using the standard alphanumeric code of A = 1,
B = 2, and so on, what word is represented by the
sequence 3 1 2 1 2 5?

Answers on pages 63 & 64.

4.
BIRD WATCHER

A cat watched a bird fly back and forth. Finally, the cat could take it no more. Seeing its chance, the cat jumped … and caught the bird in mid-flight. Nearby rescuers arrived only seconds later. Although the cat had no time to harm the bird, it was not alive. What had happened?

8

Answer on page 64.

5.
TAKING NOTES

The diagram below describes what common three-word expression?

Answer on page 64.

6.
BRICK BY BRICK

The diagram below shows one face of a chimney. No bricks were cut to form the chimney; the "half-bricks" are the ends of bricks that extend along one of the other sides. How many bricks were needed to build the entire chimney?

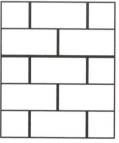

Answer on pages 64–65.

7.
TWO FOR ONE

For each pair of words or expressions below, there is a single word definition (or crossword clue) for both of them. Can you find the definitions?

MOROSE	GROSS	HOT DOG	BALL
INDIGO	MAJOR	CANDID	BEEF

Answer on page 65.

8.
FIVE OF A KIND

A) A puzzle book once challenged its readers to form an expression using five 3's so that the result would be 37. No problem: 33 + 3 + 3/3 does the trick. But can you find another way?

B) Similarly 44 + 44/4 = 55. But can you form 55 using five 4's in a completely different way?

Answers on page 65.

9.
HALF A SHAKE

If two earthquakes are a point apart on the Richter scale, then the one with the higher reading is ten times as powerful as the other. Suppose that two earthquakes differ by half a point. How much more powerful is the one with the higher reading?

10.

IN THE MIDDLE

What words contain the following letter sequences? (There may be multiple solutions. How many can you find?)

ILLILI   HTH   IQUA   AWB

Answers on pages 65 & 65–66.

11.
SURE THING

A woman wants to surprise her husband with a new ride-on mower for Christmas, which is still several days away. Unfortunately, the only place to put the new mower is in a tool shed. It is secured by a combination lock, but her husband of course knows the combination. Nonetheless, she has the store deliver the mower to the shed, and on Christmas morning has her husband open the lock, certain that he wasn't aware that a new mower was inside. How could she be so sure?

Answer on page 66.

12.
CLOSE QUARTERS

Place a quarter on a table or flat surface. Place another quarter to the right, just touching the first one. Keep going around in a circle, with each new quarter touching the center one and the one just placed. By the time you complete the circle, how many quarters will you have placed around the middle one?

Answer on page 66.

13.
BASE TEN

Suppose the numerical pyramid below kept on going.
What would be the sum of the numbers in the 10th row?

$$1$$

$$3 \qquad 5$$

$$7 \qquad 9 \qquad 11$$

$$13 \qquad 15 \qquad 17 \qquad 19$$

Answer on page 67.

14.
SEEING STARS

Each of the actors or actresses in the left-hand column can be paired with one of the musical groups or single artists in the right-hand column. Can you find the rule that brings these performers together?

Diahann Carroll	Harry Chapin
Alex Trebek	The Beatles
Jimmy Walker	The Rolling Stones
Danny DeVito	The Greg Kihn Band
Donna Pescow	Chic

Answer on page 67.

15.
DOUBLE CROSS #1

Create two independent solutions to the following mini-crossword:

ACROSS

1 Colorado, Missouri, or Mississippi

3 Tooth _____

DOWN

1 Inflexible

2 Anagram of "layer"

Answer on page 68.

Solution 1

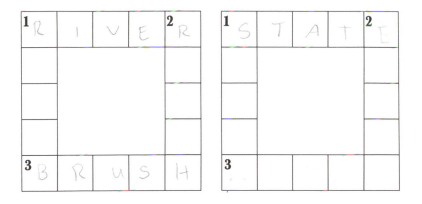

Solution 2

19

16.
ICE FOLLIES

Suppose a women's figure skating competition is held between five skaters. A skater's score equals her placement (1 through 5) in the short program multiplied by ½, plus her placement in the long program. For example, if a skater finishes fourth in the short program and third in the long program, her total score would be $4(½) + 3 = 5$. In case of a tie, the skater who did better in the long program wins.

Let's suppose, now, that the order for the short program was A, B, C, D, and E. It turns out that after the long program, there was a three-way tie for first place. Who won?

Answer on pages 68–69.

17.
ENDLESS SUMMER

Suppose that the song "99 Bottles of Beer on the Wall" was sung from beginning to end. What would be the sum of all the numbers (including repeats) in the song?

18.
FENDER BENDER

Two cars traveling on Warren Street had each just passed Redington Road when they had an accident. Remarkably, both cars sustained damage to their *front* fenders. How is this possible?

Answers on pages 69 & 70.

19.

CHECKERBOARD SQUARE

Below is a 2 by 2 checkerboard, in which four gray oversized checkers have been placed: The diameter of each checker is equal to the length of a square.

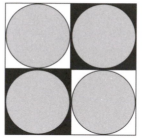

How many such checkers fit inside a standard 8×8 board?

Answer on page 70.

20.

SIGN OF THE TIMES

There are infinitely many pairs of numbers whose sum equals their product. But there is one only solution to the pair of equations below, assuming that A, B, C, D, and E each stand for a single, distinct digit.

$$AB \times C.DE = AB + C.DE$$

Can you find the solution?

Answer on pages 70–71.

21.
ODD MAN OUT

The following four men all have the three letters LEN somewhere in their names. Which one does not belong?

JAY LENO

VLADIMIR LENIN

LEN DEIGHTON

STEVE ALLEN

Answer on page 71.

22.
HIDDEN PATTERN

What do the following four seven-letter words have in common?

REALIGN   SHALLOT

CHARRED   INDULGE

23.
TIME WARP

Under what circumstances could the time in a state bordering the Atlantic be the same as the time in a state bordering the Pacific?

Answers on pages 71 & 71–72.

24.
SPEED DIALING

One morning a housewife calls her husband from their home and asks him if he wants to go out to dinner that evening. He says "Yes," so she says she'll call the restaurant to confirm a time. They hang up, and she calls the restaurant to make sure that 7:30 is okay. When she calls her husband back, she uses the redial button, even though she had called the restaurant in between. How is this possible?

(Assume that both the husband and the restaurant had caller ID, and that the same number showed up—meaning that no cell phone or second line was involved.)

Answer on page 72.

25.
A PERFECT STRANGER

A woman went into town carrying an object in her right hand. Before she had reached her destination, a man came up to her and asked, "Can I take that?" She said, "Please do," even though the man was a total stranger. What did the woman have in her hand?

Answer on page 73.

A SECOND KIND OF CUT

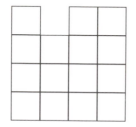

The diagram at left is a 4 by 4 grid with a square cut out. The shape can be separated into two pieces of the same shape (though of different sizes), as shown below.

Can you think of an entirely different way of dividing the shape into two pieces of the same shape? (The divisions do not all have to be along the grid lines.)

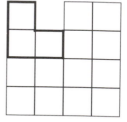

Answer on page 73.

27.
ATTENTION SPORTS FANS

What number belongs in the slot with the question mark?

1	2	3	4	5	6	7	8	9	10
0	1	1	1	1	3	2	4	4	?

Answer on pages 73–74.

28.
SHOW TIME

Place a letter in each of the eight boxes below to form three three-letter TV shows:

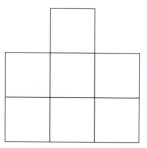

Answer on page 75.

29.

WORD CHAIN

Insert words into the blanks to create a chain of two-word expressions or compound words beginning with KEY and ending with HORSE, then the other way around:

KEY HORSE

— — — — — — — —

— — — — — — — — — —

— — — — — — — — — — — —

— — — — — — — — — — —

— — — — — — — —

HORSE — — —

KEY

Answer on page 75.

30.
HAPPY ANNIVERSARY

A summer camp was started in 1965. The owner staged a big celebration for his 35th season running the camp. In which century did that celebration take place—the 20th or the 21st?

31.
SHORT BUT SWEET

What is the smallest number of pitches that a pitcher can pitch and still come away with a complete game? (A *real* complete game; nothing rain-shortened or anything like that.)

Answers on pages 75 & 75–76.

32.

PICKING UP STICKS

A) Suppose you had five sticks of lengths 1, 2, 3, 4, and 5 inches. If you chose three of them at random, what is the likelihood that the three sticks could be put together, tip to tip, so as to form a triangle?

B) Now suppose you had twenty sticks, of lengths 1 through 20 inches. If you picked three at random, what is the likelihood that the three could be put together, tip to tip, so as to form a right triangle?

Answer on pages 76–77.

33.
ROMAN CROSSWORD

This crossword has no numbers for the clues, but plenty of numbers in the entries themselves. Every entry is either a word or a number in Roman numeral form.

Answer on page 77.

The clues are in no particular order:
The trick is to figure out where everything goes!

ACROSS		DOWN	
Words	**Numbers**	**Words**	**Numbers**
Really angry	151	Fort _____	3
Type of pride	1910	Actress	56
Poorly lit	4	Kennedy	1600
Doogie	21	Mingle	2009
Howser, _____	69	"Courteous"	52
Type of	905	war?	150
audio file	2003	Morrow	2015
	1155	Pickle type	706
	60		2200
	2		1011
	1901		2060
	3000		6
	160		1110
	156		

34.
STAYING THE SAME

No one could argue with the following equation:

$$\sqrt{10} - 3 = \sqrt{10} - 3$$

But can you add three lines to the right side of the equation so that the equation still holds true?

Answer on page 78.

35.
ALL WET

A couple went for a drive with the sunroof wide open. They kept the sunroof open even though a thunderstorm erupted, and they didn't get wet.

Another driver happened to see that peculiar sight and opened his sunroof—only to get soaking wet a short while later. Care to explain?

Answer on page 78.

36.
SPACE SAVERS

What do the eight following three-letter words have in common?

f a t	o a k	l a x	s a t
d e n	s e a	p i t	l i t

37.
THE MAX FACTOR

When the bleachers at a high school basketball game were filled to capacity, they held 319 people. Assuming that each row contained the same number of people, how many rows were there?

Answers on pages 78 & 78–79.

38.

ON THE LINE

A basketball player who makes 80 percent of his free throws goes to the foul line near the end of a very close game: His team trails by two with just 1.7 seconds remaining. If he makes both of his foul shots, the game will go into overtime.

What is the probability that he will make only one of two?

Answer on page 79.

39.
QUIT WHILE YOU'RE AHEAD

Two men are playing Russian roulette using a pistol with six chambers. Assuming that a single bullet is used and that the cylinder is spun after every turn, what is the probability that the first man will lose the game?

40.
BINARY OPERATION

What is the smallest number consisting of only 0's and 1's that is divisible by 15?

Answers on page 80.

41.
GETTING SHEEPISH

This one's been around but hasn't gotten the attention it deserves. We start with a one-acre tract of land shaped like a right triangle. At the midpoint of the hypotenuse is a post, to which a dog is tethered with a rope just long enough to reach the endpoints of the hypotenuse. There are also posts at each of the midpoints of the other two legs of the triangle; each has a post, and to each post is tethered a sheep. Again, the ropes are just long enough to permit both sheep to reach the endpoints of their respective legs.

The question is this: In how much space outside the original tract of land can the sheep graze without having to worry about the dog reaching them?

Answer on page 81.

42.
DOUBLE CROSS #2

If you liked puzzle #15, here's your second chance. Create two independent solutions to the following mini-crossword:

ACROSS

1 Caesar, for one
3 Grout and mortar guy

DOWN

1 ___ whale
2 Anagram of "dinar"

Answer on page 82.

Solution 1

Solution 2

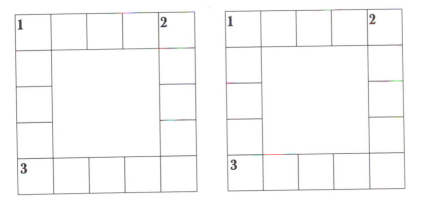

43.
CIRCULAR REASONING

If three points are placed at random around the circumference of a circle, what is the probability that all three will reside in some semi-circle, as in the diagram below?

Answer on pages 82–84.

44.
NORSE CODE

What four-letter man's name has the same property as each of the two and three-letter combinations below?

ga   sli   smo   wi   bo   la   fea

45.
BACK AND FORTH

Take a two-digit number. Square it. Reverse the three (distinct) digits of its square. Take the square root. Reverse the two digits of that number, and you have the original two-digit number. What is that number?

Answers on pages 84 & 84–85.

46.
BUMPER CROP

A farmer tells his son to select five watermelons to bring to town to be sold at the weekly farmer's market. Because the watermelons are sold by weight, they must be put on a scale before the trip into town, but the son makes a teensy-weensy mistake. Instead of weighing them individually, he weighs them in pairs. These are the weights he comes up with, in pounds:

$$20, 22, 23, 24, 25, 26, 27, 28, 30, 31$$

How much does each of the watermelons weigh?

Answer on pages 85–86.

47.

TWO GUYS

You may never have noticed, but the word "melted" consists of two men's first names placed back-to-back. Now it's your turn. Put together two men's names to form:

1) a fish
2) a flower
3) a type of shampoo
4) a carom
5) a Canadian city

Answer on page 87.

48.
DON'T FEEL STUMPED

The diagram below shows an evergreen tree. As it happens, the shape of the tree makes it possible to draw a circle around the tree as shown. How tall is the stump of the tree in relation to the entire tree?

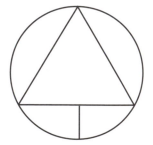

Answer on page 87.

49.

SQUARE DEAL

Imagine a 24 by 24 chessboard. Suppose you started counting all of the "sub-squares" of the chessboard: squares of lengths 1 through 24 found by tracing the sides of the squares of the big board. To remind you how many sub-squares you've counted, you make a pile of little squares (which you just happen to have around), one little square for each sub-square. It turns out that these little squares can be put together to form an even bigger square chessboard. What is the length of each side of this gigantic board?

Answer on page 88.

50.
OUT OF SIGHT

The name of Candice Bergen contains the hidden word "iceberg." Can you find the celebrities whose names contain the following hidden words?

NONE

MARSH

LIEN

Answer on page 89.

51.
THE DATING GAME

The date July 14, 1998 has the property that when written out in numeric form—i.e., 7/14/98—the year equals the product of the day and month. During the 1950s, which years had no dates of this form?

1953

1959

Answer on page 89.

52.
WHAT'S IN A NAME?

The actress Lee Grant has a name consisting of two Civil War generals. What actor or actress has a name consisting of:

1) two presidents?
2) two New York City mayors?
3) two cowboy portrayers?

Answer on page 89.

52

53.

NOT-SO-TRUE CRIME

The murder weapon was a rifle, but the victim was not shot. The cause of death was asphyxiation. A clever plot, but can you bring the perpetrator to justice? What in the world happened?

Answer on page 90.

54.
ROADS SCHOLARSHIP

Finish this story by filling in each blank with the name of a U.S. college or university.

A reckless driver had caused an accident on a _____ highway. Unfortunately for him, he was booked by the nastiest _____ police history. The driver tried to make excuses: "With all that fog, I couldn't _____ thing out there, and the rain made me _____." At that point, the man in blue responded angrily, "Look, mister, either you make _____ spend the night in jail."

Answer on page 90.

55.

MORE FUN WITH DATES

A set of three whole numbers {A, B, C} that satisfies the equation $A^2 + B^2 = C^2$ is called a Pythagorean triple. (The Pythagorean Theorem states that the three legs of any right triangle must satisfy that equation.)

What will be the last date in the 21st century that, when written out in Month/Day/Year notation, forms a Pythagorean triple? Note that March 4th, 2005 (3/04/05) is one such date, because $3^2 + 4^2 = 5^2$. However, it is not the last date in the century to fit the bill. Can you find that date?

Answer on page 91.

56.
THE BLACK HOLE

The pieces in the upper left diagram have been rearranged and placed in the lower right diagram. What happened to the hole?

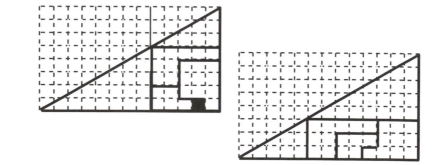

Answer on page 91.

SWEET SIXTEEN

Arrange the numbers from 1 through 16 in a 4 by 4 square such that the sum of each of the four columns is the same. (There is more than one solution.)

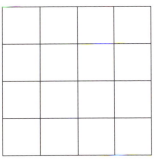

Answer on page 92.

58.
NO RULER NEEDED

Below are three quarter-circles, each of which is divided into two equal areas by a straight line. Which line is the longest? The shortest?

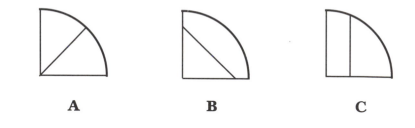

A   **B**   **C**

Answer on pages 92–93.

59.

TOUGH NEIGHBORHOOD

Place the digits 1 through 8 in the boxes below so that no two consecutive numbers are in bordering boxes.

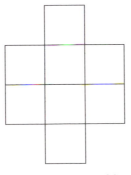

Answer on page 93.

60.
WHAT NOW?

Consider the listing of ten words given at right:

Gown
Jab
Trajectory
Jam
Jump
Jacquard
Ajar
Movable
Which
Jet

Which word comes next?
1) javelin   2) muffin
3) jackpot   4) ziti

Answer on pages 93–94.

61.
CUTTING CORNERS

The rectangle in the corner is twice as long as it is wide.
How many of these rectangles will fit in the square?

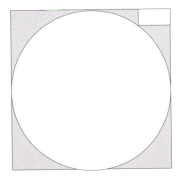

Answer on pages 94–95.

62.
OPEN AND SHUT CASE

A man lived by himself in a house with a very small bathroom. Things were so crowded in the bathroom that one of the drawers to the vanity wouldn't open all the way unless you put in some extra effort. However, every couple of weeks or so, the drawer could be pulled out quite easily. What was the problem?

Answer on page 95.

ANSWERS

1. THE HARD WAY

```
P  A  S  S  E  R
P  A  S  S  E  R
P  A  S  S  R  E
P  A  S  R  S  E
P  S  A  R  S  E
S  P  A  R  S  E
```

The key is that the first (or second) move must be to switch the two S's. That's because the indicated permutation is an even permutation that must be accomplished in an odd number of moves.

2. WHO'S NEXT?

17, 19, 23, 29, **31**
or 17, 19, 23, 29, **37**

In the first case, the listing is just a partial listing of prime numbers, and 31 is the next on the list.

In the second case, the gap between each successive member of the sequence is growing (2, 4, 6) so the next member must be 29 + 8, or 37.

3. CODE DEPENDENCE

If you write 3 1 2 1 2 5 as 3 1 2 12 5, you get CABLE. If you write it as 3 12 1 25, you get CLAY!

4. BIRD WATCHER

The cat's hunting instinct had been activated, and sorely tested, by nearby activity, so it attacked the bird—momentarily interrupting a badminton game.

5. TAKING NOTES

Face the music.

6. BRICK BY BRICK

A total of 30 bricks would be needed to make the chimney; five rows of six apiece. See illustration.

Note that the aerial view of the chimney looks like this:

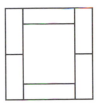

7. TWO FOR ONE

Blue   MOROSE, INDIGO
Rank   GROSS, MAJOR
Frank   HOT DOG, CANDID
Ground ___   BALL, BEEF

8. FIVE OF A KIND

$(333/3)/3 = 37$
$4! + 4! + (4! + 4)/4 = 55$

9. HALF A SHAKE

Not five! The earthquake with the higher reading is more powerful by a factor of the square root of 10, or just under 3.2.

10. IN THE MIDDLE

milliliter; lighthouse
(also eighth, lighthearted, ichthyosaur, diphthong,

knighthood), piquant (also antiquated, reliquary); and jawbone (also drawback, jawbreaker, sawbuck, lawbreaker).

11. SURE THING

As the same time as she bought the mower, she simply also picked up a new combination lock. She placed it on the shed for the week and, on Christmas Eve, she put the original lock back into place.

12. CLOSE QUARTERS

Six. When you place three quarters in the manner shown below (the gray circle is the quarter in the middle), the centers of the three quarters form the vertices of an equilateral triangle. Each angle of this triangle must be 60 degrees, so the complete 360-degree circle will accommodate six such triangles.

13. BASE TEN

The sum of the numbers in the tenth row would be 1,000. Observe that the sums of rows 1, 2, and 3 are 1, 8, and 27 respectively. In each case, the sum equals the cube of the row number, and that pattern continues. The sum of the tenth row therefore equals 10 cubed, or 1,000.

14. SEEING STARS

Each of the actors and actresses starred in a TV show that was also the name of a song. The group or musical performer who did that song is given here in parenthesis.

Julia: Diahann Carroll
(The Beatles)
Jeopardy: Alex Trebek
(The Greg Kihn Band)
Taxi: Danny Devito
(Harry Chapin)
Good Times: Jimmy Walker
(Chic)
Angie: Donna Pescow
(The Rolling Stones)

15. DOUBLE CROSS

S	T	A	T	E
T				A
I	Solution 1			R
F				L
F	A	I	R	Y

Solution 1

R	I	V	E	R
I				E
G	Solution 2			L
I				A
D	E	C	A	Y

Solution 2

16. ICE FOLLIES

Skater E is the winner. To see why, note that skaters B and D would have received one and two points, respectively, for the short program, while A, C, and E would have received 0.5, 1.5, and 2.5 points, respectively. Because the score for the long program is a whole number, the only possible three-way tie would be between skaters A, C, and E. But the only way for that to happen would be for skater E to win the long program; in that case, according to the tie-breaking rules, she would win the entire competition.

17. ENDLESS SUMMER

14,850. Begin with the verse "99 bottles of beer on the wall, 99 bottles of beer, take 1 down, pass it around, 98 bottles of beer on the wall." The numbers of the song can be displayed as follows:

99	99	1	98
98	98	1	97
97	97	1	96
.	.	.	.
3	3	1	2
2	2	1	1
1	1	1	0

The sum of the third column is 99. If that 99 is placed atop the fourth column, we see that the total sum is three times the sum of the positive integers from 1 through 99. But that sum equals (99 × 100)/2, so the total sum equals 99 × 150 = 14,850.

18. FENDER BENDER

The accident could be explained by a layout such as the one below, in which Redington Road forms a loop that comes back to meet Warren Street:

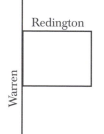

19. CHECKERBOARD SQUARE

68 circles will fit, as long as you alternate the columns.

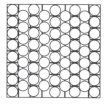

20. SIGN OF THE TIMES

$26 \times 1.04 = 26 + 1.04 = 27.04$. In general, any pair of numbers of the form X, X/(X–1) has the property that the sum equals the product: (3, 3/2), (4, 4/3), and so on. The solution to this problem is 26, 26/25.

21. ODD MAN OUT

All four men also have numbers hidden in their names, either forward or backward. In Steve Allen's case, there are two—but the letters aren't together.

Jay LENO
Vladimir LENIN
Len DEIGHTon
(S)T(Eve) Alle(N)

22. HIDDEN PATTERN

If you start with the first letter of each word and count every other letter, the result is also a word:

Re**A**l**I**g**N**
Sh**A**l**L**o**T**
Ch**A**r**R**e**D**
In**D**u**L**g**E**

23. TIME WARP

A section of Western Florida (including Pensacola) is in the Central Time Zone. A section of Oregon (including Ontario,

OR) is in the Mountain Time Zone, only one hour apart. Those two areas will have the same time for one hour at the end of daylight savings time, because clocks "fall back" at 2:00 a.m. one Sunday morning, and that time moves from east to west. So, for the hour until the end of daylight savings time in the Mountain Time Zone, Pensacola, FL, and Ontario, OR, will show the same time.

24. SPEED DIALING

One scenario is that the wife had been calling from upstairs, then went downstairs to get the phone number of the restaurant. She then called the restaurant from the kitchen phone, later calling her husband from the upstairs (i.e., bedroom) phone. The point is that the redial button is specific to the actual handset, and doesn't apply to the entire line.

25. A PERFECT STRANGER

She was carrying a letter and was on her way to the closest mailbox. The man in question was a postman.

26. A SECOND KIND OF CUT

The diagram at left creates two pieces of the same shape, as long as the vertical lines at the left and right of the smaller piece are made at points two-thirds of the way along their respective squares. (This dissection is the creation of Michael Reid. It's a beauty!)

27. ATTENTION SPORTS FANS

1	2	3	4	5	6	7	8	9	10
0	1	1	1	1	3	2	4	4	5

The numbers in the nth column of the second row give the number of distinct ways of scoring n points in football. Here is the complete list:

Points / Method

1 / Impossible
2 / Safety
3 / Field goal
4 / Two safeties
5 / Field goal and safety
6 / Two field goals; three safeties; one touchdown
7 / A field goal and two safeties; a touchdown with extra point
8 / Four safeties; two field goals and a safety; a touchdown and a safety; a touchdown plus two-point conversion
9 / Three field goals; a touchdown and a field goal; a touchdown with extra point and a safety; a field goal and three safeties.
10 / A touchdown with an extra point and a field goal; five safeties; two safeties and two field goals; a touchdown and two safeties; a touchdown with a two-point conversion and a safety.

28. SHOW TIME

29. WORD CHAIN

KEY
CHAIN
LETTER
PERFECT
PITCH
DARK
HORSE

HORSE
FLY
BALL
POINT
BLANK
CHECK
OFF
KEY

30. HAPPY ANNIVERSARY

The 35th season of the camp took place in 1999, not 2000, so it definitely took place in the 20th century, whether you consider the 21st century to have begun on January 1, 2000 or January 1, 2001.

31. SHORT BUT SWEET

25 pitches would be enough, in theory—and only on the assumption that the pitcher was pitching for the away

team! The way this could happen is if every batter swung at the first pitch, with 24 out of 25 hitting into an out and the other one hitting a home run. Assuming that the pitcher's team never scored at all, the final score would be 1–0 in favor of the home team, which then wouldn't have to bat in the last half of the ninth inning. (Thanks to "Test Your Baseball Literacy," by R. Wayne Schmittberger, for suggesting this little gem.)

32. PICKING UP STICKS

A) For the first problem, there are 10 ways of choosing the three sticks (five choices for the first, four for the second, and three for the third, but you have to divide by six—the number of ways of rearranging the three chosen sticks—because a choice of, say, 2–4–5 yields the same triangle as a choice of 5–2–4). Of those ten ways of choosing three sticks, only three result in triangles: 2–3–4, 2–4–5, and 3–4–5. That's because the sum of any two sides must be greater than the third side.

B) For the second problem, there are 1,140 ways of choosing the three sticks: (20 × 19 × 18)/6. But only these six combinations satisfy the Pythagorean Theorem: 3–4–5, 6–8–10, 9–12–15, 12–16–20, 5–12–13, and 8–15–17. The chance of

creating a right triangle is therefore 6/1140 = 1/190.

33. ROMAN CROSSWORD

34. STAYING THE SAME

$$\sqrt{10} - 3 = \sqrt{\dfrac{1}{10 + 3}}$$

35. ALL WET

As long as you maintain a high enough speed, a wind foil will form across the top of the sunroof opening, keeping the passengers dry. But the foil doesn't operate at low rates of speed; when the second driver slowed down, the rain came pouring in.

36. SPACE SAVERS

Each of the eight three-letter words is an abbreviation for a U.S. airport:

FAT   Fresno
OAK   Oakland
LAX   Los Angeles
SAT   San Antonio
DEN   Denver
SEA   Seattle
PIT   Pittsburgh
LIT   Little Rock

37. THE MAX FACTOR

There were 11 rows. The conditions of the problem

suggest that 319 is a composite number, and in fact $319 = 11 \times 29$. Eleven rows of 29 people would be much more likely than 29 rows of 11 people!

38. ON THE LINE

The probability that the player will make only one free throw is slightly more than 4/25. If he makes his first one (probability 4/5) and misses his second one (probability 1/5), we get a compound probability of $(4/5)(1/5) = 4/25$. But if he missed the first free throw, he will try to miss the second one so that he or a teammate can put in the rebound. (There is no sense in making the second free throw, because the opponents would then have the ball with a one-point lead and only 1.7 seconds on the clock. The reason that the final probability is slightly more than 4/25 is that the player, in deliberately trying to miss his second free throw, might screw up and put it in the basket!

39. QUIT WHILE YOU'RE AHEAD

The probability that the first player will lose the game equals 6/11. To see why, note that there is a 1/6 chance that he will lose on his first shot. On the other hand, there is a 25/36 probability that he will get to shoot again, because that is the probability that both he and his opponent will miss their first shots. At that point, the game essentially starts over again. Putting all this into an equation, we get P = 1/6 + (25/36)P, so (11/36)P = 1/6 and P = 6/11.

40. BINARY OPERATION

For a number to be divisible by 15 it must be divisible by both 3 and 5. A number is divisible by 3 if and only if the sum of its digits is divisible by 3, so the number in question, consisting of only 0's and 1's, must have three 1's in it. Add a zero and we get our answer: 1,110.

41. GETTING SHEEPISH

The area that the sheep have to themselves is precisely one acre. To account for this surprising result, check out the diagram. The big circle indicates the area available to the dog. (Note that the big circle must intersect with the third vertex of

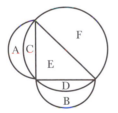

the triangle because it is a right triangle.) By using the Pythagorean Theorem and the formula $A = \pi r^2$ for a circle, we see that the area of the two smaller semi-circles must equal the area of the larger semi-circle, so $A + C + B + D = F$. But $F = C + E + D$, so we have $A + C + B + D = C + E + D$ and therefore $A + B = E$. We know that E equals one acre, and $A + B$ is the area that the sheep have to themselves, so that does it.

42. DOUBLE CROSS #2

S	A	L	A	D
P				R
E	Solution	1		A
R				I
M	A	S	O	N

Solution 1

R	O	M	A	N
I				A
G	Solution	2		D
H				I
T	I	L	E	R

Solution 2

43. CIRCULAR REASONING

The probability is ¾. To see why, first position a point at the bottom of a circle. Then imagine a second point starting at the bottom and traveling clockwise around the circumference.

With the second point at the starting point, the third point could be placed anywhere on the circle and the three points would have to be in a common semi-circle. As the second point starts its clockwise journey, the options for the third point would shrink somewhat; specifically, if x denotes the number of degrees traveled by the second point, then the third point could be placed anywhere within an arc of $360 - x$ degrees to ensure that the three points would all fit in a semi-circle. This pattern would continue until the second point was at the very top of the circle (when, technically, the third point could again be placed anywhere), and then the pattern would reverse itself as the second point traveled down the right side of the circle. For any value between 0 and 360 (for the second point), the lined area of the diagram that follows indicates the possibilities for the second point to satisfy the semi-circle condition. You will note that the lined area is precisely 3/4 the size of the square. That does it!

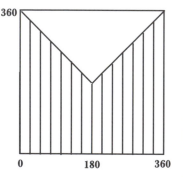

44. NORSE CODE

The answer is Eric, as in Eric *the Red.* Note that each of the nonsense combinations makes sense when attached to ___thered:

gathered, **sli**thered, **smo**thered, **wi**thered, **bo**thered, **la**thered, **fea**thered

45. BACK AND FORTH

The original number was 13. Squaring it gives 169. Reverse that to get 961, and take the square root to get 31. Another reversal gets you back from where you started.

46. BUMPER CROP

From lightest to heaviest, the watermelons weigh 9, 11, 13, 14, and 17 pounds.

The first step in solving is to note that there are six even combinations of weights (20, 22, 24, 26, 28, and 30) and four odd combinations (23, 25, 27, and 31).

Even combinations must be made up of two weights that are both even or both odd (or, in math-speak, have the same parity), while odd combos must have one of each. Since all ten combinations aren't the same parity, the weights aren't all odd or all even.

If the weights aren't all the same, they must be broken up into sets of 1 and 4, or 2 and 3. Say it's 2 and 3. It doesn't matter which is even and odd;

let's call one group A and the other group B. The ten pairings of A, A, B, B, and B are one AA, six ABs, and three BBs. Matching pairs are even and differing pairs are odd, which makes four even and six odd. We know there are actually six even and four odd, so the distribution must be 1 and 4. Calling the groups A and B again, this means the four odd combinations all result from the single A weight paired in turn with the four B weights.

Those totals are 23, 25, 27, and 31, so if we call the lightest B weight x, the four B weights equal x, $x+2$, $x+4$, and $x+8$. Those four weights combine to make the six even totals, which means $2x+2$, $2x+4$, $2x+6$, $2x+8$, $2x+10$, and $2x+12$ are equal to 20, 22, 24, 26, 28, and 30, respectively. It's easy now to determine that x must equal 9, and with that information we now know the five weights are 9, 11, 13, 14, and 17.

47. TWO GUYS

Skipjack
Stephanotis
Herbal
Ricochet
Calgary

48. DON'T FEEL STUMPED

By drawing additional lines, we divide the equilateral triangle into six congruent right triangles. Because these triangles are all "30-60-90" triangles (the measures of the three angles), in each case the shorter side is equal to one-half the hypotenuse. But we also know that these triangles meet at the center of the circle, so the "stump" of the tree must equal half the radius, or one-fourth the total height of the tree.

49. SQUARE DEAL

The answer is 70. To count the number of sub-squares on a 24 by 24 chessboard, it helps to look first at a 3 by 3 case.

 In a 3 by 3 chessboard, there are 9 squares of size 1 by 1, 4 squares of size 2 by 2 (each of the 4 squares in the 2 by 2 square at the bottom left could itself be the bottom left square for a 2 by 2 sub-square!), and, of course, 1 square of size 3 by 3, for a total of 13.

In general, the number of sub-squares on an n by n chessboard equals the sum of all squares less than or equal to n, which is given by the formula $n(n + 1)(2n + 1)/6$.

For n = 24, the number of sub-squares equals 24(25)(49)/6, or 4,900.

This is 70^2, so the side of the big chessboard must be 70 squares long.

50. OUT OF SIGHT

ryaN O'NEal
oMAR SHarif
wilLIE Nelson
(or juLIE Newmar)

51. THE DATING GAME

1953, 1958, and 1959. Note that 53 and 59 are prime numbers, and no prime years after 1931 have the desired property (January 31, 1931 = 1/31/31).

Although 58 is not prime, its prime factorization is 2 × 29, and 2/29/58 does not work because 1958 was not a leap year: There was no February 29, 1958!

52. WHAT'S IN A NAME?

Two presidents:
  Harrison Ford
Two New York City mayors:
  Lindsay Wagner
Two cowboy portrayers:
  Wayne Rogers

53. NOT-SO-TRUE CRIME

The crime was committed near the slopes of a mountain. The victim was snow-shoeing alongside the mountain when the perpetrator fired his shotgun, starting a fatal avalanche.

54. ROADS SCHOLARSHIP

A reckless driver had caused an accident on a TULANE highway. Unfortunately for him, he was booked by the nastiest COPPIN STATE police history. The driver tried to make excuses: "With all that fog, I couldn't SIENA thing out there, and the rain made me SKIDMORE." At that point the man in blue responded angrily, "Look, mister, either you make BAYLOR spend the night in jail."

55. MORE FUN WITH DATES

The date in question is October 24th, 2026, or 10/24/26.

56. THE BLACK HOLE

The black hole didn't go anywhere: The illusion is caused by the fact that the two big "triangles" are not in fact the same shape.

Note, in the drawings at right, that the slope of the top triangle in the top diagram is 3/5, whereas the slope of the other triangle in that diagram is 5/8. The slight difference (0.6 versus 0.625) is barely noticeable to the eye, but it means that the whole "triangle" actually bulges slightly.

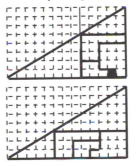

57. SWEET SIXTEEN

The left diagram below shows one arrangement where the columns all have equal sums. The way to produce this solution is to first create the diagram on the right, in which the digits 1 2, 3, 4 have been staggered both horizontally and vertically. Clearly the columns of this diagram have equal sums, and the left-hand diagram is obtained by adding 0, 4, 8, and 12 to rows one, two, three, and four, respectively, and these operations keep the column sums equal.

1	2	3	4
8	5	6	7
11	12	9	10
14	15	16	13

1	2	3	4
4	1	2	3
3	4	1	2
2	3	4	1

58. NO RULER NEEDED

Line B is the longest, A is in the middle, and C is the shortest. To see why B is longer than A, we draw a couple of extra lines, as seen here, showing that the line in B exceeds the radius of the circle. But the line in C is shorter than the radius of the circle, so A is in the middle.

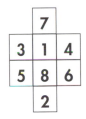

A

B

C

59. TOUGH NEIGHBORHOOD

Here is one solution:

	7	
3	1	4
5	8	6
	2	

60. WHAT NOW?

3. The ten words contain the initials of the first ten presidents, as follows:

George Washington (GoWn)

John Adams (JAb)

Thomas Jefferson (TraJectory)

James Madison (JaM)

James Monroe (JuMp)

John Quincy Adams (JacQuArd)

Andrew Jackson (AJar)

Martin Van Buren (MoVaBle)

William Henry Harrison (WHicH)

John Tyler (JeT)

The initials of the eleventh president, James Knox Polk, are found in JacKPot.

61. CUTTING CORNERS

50. By drawing a few lines, we see that the radius must be the hypotenuse of a right triangle, as below. Note that the three sides of the right triangle form an arithmetic progression with a difference of d between consecutive pairs. The only

triangle that satisfies this condition is the triangle (3d, 4d, 5d), so the radius is 5d. Each side of the square is therefore 10d, so 50 of the little rectangles fit in the square.

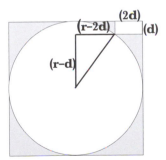

62. OPEN AND SHUT CASE

The problem was that the toilet paper holder blocked the drawer—at least when the roll was mostly full. By the time the roll had wound down a good part of the way, it no longer blocked the drawer.

ABOUT THE AUTHOR

DERRICK NIEDERMAN is the author of *The Little Giant Book of Math Puzzles*, *Hard-to-Solve Math Puzzles*, and *Math Puzzles for the Clever Mind*. When not writing puzzle books (which isn't very often), he writes about mathematics and finance. His books include *A Killing on Wall Street* and, with David Boyum, *What the Numbers Say: A Field Guide to Mastering Our Numerical World*.

Niederman lives in Needham, Massachusetts.